## YOU CHOOSE

# CAN YOU ESCAPE A HAUNTED HOTEL?

## AN INTERACTIVE PARANORMAL ADVENTURE

BY MEGAN COOLEY PETERSON

CAPSTONE PRESS
a capstone imprint

Published by Capstone Press, an imprint of Capstone
1710 Roe Crest Drive, North Mankato, Minnesota 56003
capstonepub.com

Copyright © 2025 by Capstone. All rights reserved. No part of this publication may be reproduced in whole or in part, or stored in a retrieval system, or transmitted in any form or by any means, electronic, mechanical, photocopying, recording, or otherwise, without written permission of the publisher.

Library of Congress Cataloging-in-Publication Data

Names: Peterson, Megan Cooley, author.
Title: Can you escape a haunted hotel? : an interactive paranormal adventure / by Megan Cooley Peterson.
Description: North Mankato, Minnesota : Capstone Press, an imprint of Capstone, 2024. | Series: You choose: haunted adventures | Includes bibliographical references. | Audience: Ages 8 to 12. | Audience: Grades 4-6.
Summary: An interactive adventure where the reader explores haunted hotels and experiences ghostly encounters based on reported sightings around the world. Includes additional information about the hotels' haunted history.
Identifiers: LCCN 2024006143 (print) | LCCN 2024006144 (ebook) | ISBN 9781669069188 (hardcover) | ISBN 9781669069157 (paperback) | ISBN 9781669069164 (pdf) | ISBN 9781669069171 (epub)
Subjects: CYAC: Haunted places--Fiction. | Hotels, motels, etc.--Fiction. | Plot-your-own stories. | LCGFT: Choose-your-own stories.
Classification: LCC PZ7.1.P456 Cap 2024 (print) | LCC PZ7.1.P456 (ebook) | DDC [Fic]--dc23
LC record available at https://lccn.loc.gov/2024006143
LC ebook record available at https://lccn.loc.gov/2024006144

Editorial Credits
Editor: Mandy Robbins; Designer: Dina Her; Media Researcher: Jo Miller; Production Specialist: Tori Abraham

Photo Credits
Alamy: Adrian Muttitt, 23; Getty Images: LeoPatrizi, 63; Newscom: ZUMAPRESS/Joseph Kaczmarek, 58; Shutterstock: Anna Kucherova, Cover, Christele, 46, Dragos Pop, 6, Everett Collection, 44 (both), FOTOKITA, 53, Jason Valentine, 72, Mulberry C, 96, Obsidian Fantasy Studio, 50, Olivier Le Queinec, 27, Patrick Horton, 16, 20, ProCinemaStock, 68, RaksyBH, 11, 31, 100, Stella_E, 28, Surin Sergii, 98, Tom Tom, 107, tugol, 79, YAKOBCHUK VIACHESLAV, 87, Yau Ming Low, 42, zef art, 103, 106

Design Elements
Shutterstock: Nik Merkulov, Olha Nion

Any additional websites and resources referenced in this book are not maintained, authorized, or sponsored by Capstone. All product and company names are trademarks™ or registered® trademarks of their respective holders.

Printed and bound in China. 6274

# TABLE OF CONTENTS

## INTRODUCTION
ABOUT YOUR ADVENTURE ................5

## CHAPTER 1
CHECKING IN? ..........................7

## CHAPTER 2
THE CRESCENT HOTEL ..................17

## CHAPTER 3
THE LANGHAM HOTEL ...................43

## CHAPTER 4
THE FAIRMONT BANFF SPRINGS HOTEL .....73

## CHAPTER 5
HAUNTED HOTELS ..................... 101

MORE GHOSTLY ENCOUNTERS ............. 106
OTHER PATHS TO EXPLORE ............... 108
GLOSSARY............................. 109
BIBLIOGRAPHY .........................110
READ MORE............................ 111
INTERNET SITES........................ 111
ABOUT THE AUTHOR ....................112

# INTRODUCTION
# ABOUT YOUR ADVENTURE

YOU are about to travel to three different hotels around the world. Just don't expect to get much rest. Each one is said to be haunted. What would you do if you had a ghostly encounter at a hotel? It's time to find out.

Chapter One sets the scene. Then you choose which path to read. Follow the directions at the bottom of the page. Your decisions will change your outcome. After you finish one path, go back and read the others for new perspectives and more adventures.

Turn the page to begin your adventure.

# CHAPTER 1
# CHECKING IN?

"Do you enjoy traveling? Need a break from your everyday routine? Why not check into one of these lovely hotels? Each one boasts plush beds, delicious food, and stunning views. Unfortunately, a restful night's sleep can't be guaranteed. Each hotel offers something . . . a little extra. Will you be brave enough to check in?"

Turn the page.

You turn off your microphone and lean back in your office chair. You are the host of a new haunted-travel podcast called *The Dead and Breakfast*. You plan to feature the world's most haunted hotels and inns. But you're not quite sure which to include for your debut episode. With so many podcasts out there, it's hard to stand out. And you want yours to be a success.

Your family stayed at a creepy hotel when you were young. You've been obsessed with ghosts ever since. The hotel looked like an old castle. Inside, the rooms were drafty and cold. One night, you were awakened by the sound of crying. The ghostly outline of a woman floated above you. Your parents assured you it was only a bad dream. But you know what you saw—a ghost.

Suddenly, your best friend and roommate, Molly, flies in carrying her phone.

"You are not going to believe what's happening in Arkansas," she says.

"If it's not related to haunted hotels, I don't have time," you say. You already told everyone your first episode would drop next month. And so far, you're not sure which hotel to cover first.

Molly shoves her phone at you. "Read this, and then you can thank me," she says.

Sighing, you take her phone and read the headline: *MYSTERIOUS BOTTLES FOUND AT QUACK PHYSICIAN'S FORMER HOSPITAL.*

You shoot your friend a look. "My podcast is about haunted hotels, not old hospitals."

She rolls her eyes. "Just keep reading, smarty pants."

Turn the page.

As you read the rest of the article, the hairs on your neck stand up. The Crescent Hotel in Arkansas was a "hospital" back in the late 1930s. Norman Baker pretended to be a doctor who could cure cancer. He delivered fake cancer treatments, conning hundreds of people out of their money. Now a hotel groundskeeper has discovered hundreds of specimen jars buried on the property.

"This is amazing," you tell your friend. "I'm sorry I doubted you."

Molly gives you a smug smile. "Apparently, this place is one of the most haunted hotels on the planet. You've got to go there!"

She gives you a thumbs up before she heads out the door.

Your mind spins with ideas for a podcast episode about the Crescent Hotel. You could spend a night there. You start researching the hauntings. Hotel staff and visitors say ghostly patients roam the halls. The old morgue is still on site and included on a ghost tour. Will the ghost of Norman Baker himself make an appearance?

The lobby of the Crescent Hotel and Spa

Turn the page.

After a couple hours of research, you meet your parents for dinner. They just got back from a trip to London, and you can't wait to hear about it.

"London was amazing!" your mom says. "I'm so glad we finally decided to go."

"Your mom took selfies with all the royal guards at Buckingham Palace," your dad says. "I think one of them almost smiled!" Your mom laughs and playfully smacks your dad's hand.

"Where'd you stay?" you ask. You know they told you, but you forgot. You've been preoccupied with your podcast.

"This gorgeous old hotel in the West End called the Langham Hotel," your dad says.

The hotel sounds familiar. Then it hits you—the Langham Hotel came up in one of your late-night searches for haunted hotels.

"Did you have any ghostly encounters?" you ask, only half serious.

Your mom's face goes pale. "Actually, I think I did," she says. "I was in the pool late one night when I felt a presence. But there was no one around." She shudders. "Gives me the creeps just thinking about it."

As your parents read over the dessert menu, you pull out your phone. There are tons of articles and posts about hauntings at the Langham. A phantom butler has been reported by several guests. Emperor Napoleon III of France is said to haunt the basement. And the spirit of a German prince may have decided to stick around after his untimely death. Your parents have just done you a huge favor—they helped you decide on another podcast episode.

Turn the page.

Later that night, you hear a noise in your apartment, and you jump. All of your ghostly research has you spooked.

"It's only me!" Molly says. "Sorry to scare you."

You have never been so relieved to see her face. "I've found another hotel for the podcast," you say as your heartbeat returns to normal. You tell her about your parents' vacation at the Langham and your mom's ghostly encounter.

"Speaking of haunted hotels," she says, "I've got another one you can visit. My family is heading to Canada for their yearly ski trip. They said I could bring you along this time, all expenses paid."

"What's the hotel?" you ask.

"The Fairmont Banff Springs Hotel in Alberta," Molly says. "My aunt is super into ghosts, which is why she picked it. There's allegedly a ghostly bride who died on the main staircase. And the spirit of a bellman who can't stop helping the guests. Are you in?"

You're thrilled to have another option. The only question now is which haunted hotel do you want to investigate first?

- To explore the Crescent Hotel, turn to page 17.
- To visit the Langham Hotel, turn to page 43.
- To check into the Fairmont Banff Springs Hotel, turn to page 73.

# CHAPTER 2
# THE CRESCENT HOTEL

The next morning, you pack a bag and hop on a bus headed for Eureka Springs, Arkansas. The ride gives you time to read up on the history of the Crescent Hotel. In 1886, it opened as a luxury hotel. Built in the Ozark Mountains, the Crescent drew guests seeking the healing waters of the area's natural springs.

The hotel became the Crescent College and Conservatory for Young Women from 1908 to 1924. During the summer, it still operated as a resort. But the cost to maintain the Crescent was too high. The college and resort closed.

Turn the page.

In 1937, the hotel had a buyer—Norman Baker. Born in Iowa in 1882, Baker started out as a carnival performer. He invented the calliaphone, a musical instrument used for carnivals. He also started his own radio stations and a magazine, which advertised a new cure for cancer. Baker opened a cancer hospital in Iowa in 1929. But he had no medical training, and the American Medical Association spoke out against his treatments.

By 1937, Eureka Springs, Arkansas, seemed like the perfect place for Baker to open a new cancer hospital. The Baker Hospital promised to cure cancer without operations, X-rays, or radium. These promises were not cheap. Baker made millions of dollars "treating" his patients. But his "cure" was a total lie.

You look up from your research as the bus reaches the city of Eureka Springs. The hotel is nestled between green trees and rolling hills. It is five stories high and made of limestone. Turrets, balconies, and spires add to its grandeur.

In the lobby, dark wood beams crisscross the ceiling. Large windows let in lots of light. A huge stone fireplace dominates the center of the lobby. What looks like a large church organ takes up an entire wall. A sign says it's one of Norman Baker's calliaphones. The sound of soft carnival music begins to play. It seems to be coming from the instrument. But there's no one playing it. As you lean closer, the music stops.

Shaking your head, you cross to the front desk to check in. You called yesterday and booked the hotel's most haunted room.

Turn the page.

The reception desk of the Crescent Hotel and Spa

"Are you sure you want to stay in room 218?" the clerk asks, handing you a key. "I've heard it's haunted by a stonemason who died while building the hotel."

"That's exactly why I want to stay there," you explain. You tell him about your podcast featuring haunted hotels. "Do you know anything more about the ghost?"

"Only that his name was Michael," he says. "Good luck tonight. You're going to need it."

His warning seems a bit dramatic. But maybe the staff is encouraged to play up the ghost factor. As you turn toward the stairs, you notice a group of people standing together. A woman in a Victorian-style dress and top hat tells them about the various ghosts that haunt the Crescent. It's a ghost tour!

"Let's head down to the morgue," the tour guide says. "We don't want to keep our ghostly friends waiting!"

Featuring the morgue in your podcast is a must. People died in Baker's phony hospital, and their stories deserve to be told. But you're also exhausted from your trip. A quick nap sounds nice.

- To tour the morgue, turn to page 22.
- To go to room 218, turn to page 26.

The chance to tour the old morgue is too good to pass up. The tour guide leads you through a fancy spa and down an old stone corridor. Exposed pipes line the walls. A doorway leads into the musty, concrete morgue. Photographs of Norman Baker hang on the walls. His eyes seem to follow you wherever you go.

"Welcome to the morgue," the guide says. "For those of you who just joined, I'm Sally, and the stories I'm telling are all true. If you start to feel faint or need to leave, please do." Sally leads you into the next room. A shelf on the wall holds specimen jars.

"Norman Baker was a fraud," Sally tells the group. "One of his so-called cures was called Formula Five. It was made of alcohol, watermelon seeds, corn silk, glycerol, clover, and carbolic acid. It cured no one."

She says Baker's workers injected patients with this mixture several times a day. The Baker Hospital contained no actual medicine or trained medical staff.

"What about the specimen jars?" you ask, eager to learn more.

Sally nods. "Workers found around 400 jars buried on the property. Some of the jars were broken. Others still held liquid. They're still being tested. But I have a strong feeling many contain human tissue."

Gasps ring out among the group. You move closer to the jars. They contain different colored liquids, from yellow to green to brown. Some have bits of flesh inside. You shudder at the horrible display. As you turn to go, a scratching sound comes from behind the locked case of jars. It might be a rodent. Or maybe you're just tired from your trip and hearing things.

"I've saved the scariest stop in the morgue for last," Sally says. "Let's head into the cold room. This is where Baker kept the dead."

- To go into the cold room, go to the next page.
- To investigate the noise, turn to page 27.

You follow Sally. As you step into the cramped room, the temperature drops.

"The bodies of patients who died were kept in here," Sally explains. "Then they were transported for burial. No one knows exactly how many patients died at the Crescent, but some say almost fifty."

You stay until you're the last person left in the room. The tips of your fingers go numb. Your stomach hurts, and you feel dizzy. Your vision grows hazy. You need to leave now. You rush from the cold room, feeling better almost instantly. You've never had an experience like that before. Were you just nervous? Or were the ghosts of Baker's former patients in the cold room with you? You can't stop shaking and decide you need to rest.

Turn the page.

You head upstairs to room 218. You push open the glossy black door and crawl into the bed.

Your nap doesn't last long. Something knocks against your headboard, and you sit up with a jolt. You check behind the bed. There's nothing there. The bathroom is empty too. You shrug and lie back down. Suddenly, the balcony door creaks open slightly. Perhaps the wind pushed it open. Or is it the ghost of Michael, the worker who died?

Your stomach grumbles, and you can't remember the last time you ate. Should you check out the balcony or head downstairs and grab a bite to eat first? If this room is as haunted as the clerk says, Michael's ghost will still be here later.

- To investigate the balcony, turn to page 29.
- To get something to eat, turn to page 31.

You follow the noise along the wall. At the end, you find a door you hadn't noticed earlier. The sound seems to be coming from behind the door. You open it a crack and slip inside.

This room is even colder than the last one. An industrial sink is set against one wall. You swallow, trying not to imagine what Norman Baker used this room for. Maybe you should have stayed with the group.

Turn the page.

Before you can leave, the lights shut off. The room is pitch black. "Hello?" you say. There is no answer.

When the lights come back on, hospital beds fill the space. They weren't here a moment ago. A patient lies in one of them. She locks eyes with you and holds out her hand. Everything is hazy. And the woman . . . glows. You have a bad feeling this isn't part of the tour.

- To try to help the woman, turn to page 33.
- To flee, turn to page 37.

You step slowly toward the balcony door. As you reach for the handle, a shadowy figure moves outside. It vanishes the moment you step onto the empty balcony. You suddenly feel like you've been here before. The air gets colder. Fog rolls down the mountain.

The building around you changes. Scaffolding now covers the side of the uncompleted hotel. A young man above you wears a large tool belt as he works. He leans out over the side to reach for something. He loses his balance, his arms flail, and you watch with horror as he falls.

The man lands on the second-floor slab you're standing on. Someone yells, "Michael!" You want to help the man, but your body is frozen in place.

Turn the page.

Suddenly, the fog lifts. You're back standing on the empty balcony. The scaffolding is gone, along with the man you saw fall. But could Michael's ghost still be here? Maybe you could find the guide from the ghost tour. She might have more information about Michael. Or you could try communicating with him yourself.

- To find the tour guide, go to the next page.
- To try communicating with the ghost in room 218, turn to page 40.

You head for the elevator. It looks original to the building. It has a glossy black frame with gold doors. You step inside and press the button for the lobby.

The doors ding closed. Instead of going down, the elevator goes up to the fourth floor. The doors slide open. When you press the lobby button, nothing happens. *Elevator must be glitchy today*, you tell yourself before stepping onto the fourth floor. You'll just take the staircase to the lobby.

Turn the page.

Down the hall, a woman in an old-timey white dress is struggling to unlock her door. She seems flustered. You walk down the hall and stop in front of room 419.

"Hello, there," you say. "Can I help you with that?"

The woman smiles. "That would be very kind of you. This lock is always so tricky," she says. "I'm Theodora, by the way."

She gives you her key and steps aside. You unlock the door. When you turn to give her the key, she's gone. You look up and down the long hall. Theodora is nowhere to be seen. You want to make sure she gets her key back.

- To return her key to the front desk, turn to page 35.
- To search for Theodora, turn to page 39.

You force your feet toward the patient in the bed. Her skin is almost see-through.

"Please, help me," she whispers.

You frantically look around the room for medicine. All you find are jars of Formula Five. Norman Baker's "cure" won't help this woman.

A shadow moves into the room. At first, you think it's Sally the tour guide. But then it grows into a man in a lavender doctor's coat. It's Norman Baker! He twists his face into a cruel smile.

A scream rises in your throat. Someone taps your arm, and you startle. It's Sally. The beds are now gone, along with the patient.

Turn the page.

"Are you alright?" Sally asks. "You look like you've seen a ghost."

A tour group member stands next to her. He is an older gentleman who resembles Norman Baker.

You laugh nervously. "Did Norman Baker wear lavender by any chance?"

Sally's eyes widen. "He always wore lavender."

## THE END

To follow another path, turn to page 15.
To learn more about haunted hotels, turn to page 101.

You take the winding black staircase down to the lobby. The clerk who checked you in smiles.

"What can I do for you?" he asks.

You set the key to room 419 on the counter. "I'm hoping you can return this to Theodora. I was helping her into her room, but she stepped away."

The clerk's smile disappears. "You said her name was Theodora? White dress?"

"Yes," you say, curiously. "Do you know her?"

"Theodora is one of the Crescent's most popular ghosts," he says. "She was either a nurse or patient when Norman Baker owned the place. Many guests have reported her struggling with the door. She's also been seen pushing a gurney."

Turn the page.

Another hotel worker joins you at the counter. "I stayed in room 419 once," she says. "I left all my clothes on the bed. When I got back from dinner, all my things were in the dresser."

After dinner, you return to your room to write about your encounter with Theodora. But your bag is empty. With shaking hands, you slowly open your dresser drawer. Tucked away inside are all of your clothes, your notebook, and your pen.

## THE END

To follow another path, turn to page 15.
To learn more about haunted hotels, turn to page 101.

You won't stay here a moment longer. Podcast or not, the room feels unsafe. As you hurry back through the corridor, the memory of the ghostly patient grows fuzzy. Did you just imagine it? You are very hungry and feeling lightheaded. A good meal is what you need. The more you think about it, the more you're certain you were seeing things.

You enter the Crystal Dining Room. A large chandelier hangs from the ceiling. A server gives you a menu.

"Welcome to the Crescent," she says, pouring you some water. "I'll be right back for your order."

As you read the menu, something brushes against your ankles. It feels like a cat, and you have a terrible cat allergy. You flip up the tablecloth. There's no cat. But you start to feel wheezy anyway. You sneeze and cough.

Turn the page.

The server comes back to take your order. You wipe your eyes. "Is there a cat in this hotel?" you ask. "I'm terribly allergic."

The server smiles. "Yes, in a sense. Morris was the beloved hotel cat who died years back. He's buried out in the rose garden. But people see him around the hotel all of the time."

You order some food to take back to your room. As you pass through the lobby, you see the rose garden outside. Morris is the most interesting ghost you've met so far at the Crescent. But you can't risk another encounter when your allergies are this bad. When you open the door to your room, a single rose sits on the bed.

## THE END

To follow another path, turn to page 15.
To learn more about haunted hotels, turn to page 101.

The hallway stretches in both directions. Black doors line the pale-yellow halls. Ceiling fans cast strange shadows. You walk to one end of the hall and back again. Room 419 still sits open. Where could Theodora have gone?

Wheels squeak behind you. You spin around to find her pushing something. It looks like an empty hospital gurney.

"Theodora?" you ask, your voice unsteady.

"Excuse me," she says. "I've got a patient to move."

You try to step out of her way, but she pushes the gurney right through you! It feels like an icy breeze passing through you. Theodora and her gurney fade away. Your mouth grows dry as you realize she is not a guest at the Crescent at all.

## THE END

To follow another path, turn to page 15.
To learn more about haunted hotels, turn to page 101.

You slip back into room 218 and close the balcony door. Digging through your bag, you pull out your phone. You switch on your camera and start recording.

"Hello, Michael," you say. "Are you the man who fell building this hotel?"

A dresser drawer suddenly opens by itself. Your heart races, and your back breaks out in a sweat. The wind couldn't have done that. It must be Michael's ghost. The ghost doesn't seem angry. You wonder if he's lonely or afraid.

"Nice to meet you, Michael," you say, your voice shaking a little. "I'm sorry about what happened to you. Thank you for helping to build such a lovely hotel."

The drawer shuts softly. You wait for more ghostly activity, but nothing happens. You grab a notebook and start jotting down ideas for your debut episode. You pick up your phone to watch the video, but the battery is dead. When you charge it, you can't find the video.

You sleep peacefully until morning. "Rest well, Michael," you say before leaving room 218. You can almost hear someone whisper back, "Thank you."

## THE END

To follow another path, turn to page 15.
To learn more about haunted hotels, turn to page 101.

## CHAPTER 3
# THE LANGHAM HOTEL

As your plane soars over the Atlantic, you look out the window at the setting sun. You're on your way to London, England, to visit the Langham Hotel. Before you arrive, you want to learn as much as you can about the hotel.

The Langham Hotel opened in London's West End on June 10, 1865. The ownership group named the hotel for Sir James Langham, the previous owner of the land. The Prince of Wales, Edward VII, was on hand to open London's grandest hotel.

Turn the page.

Mark Twain (left) and King Edward VII (right)

For years, the Langham was the poshest hotel in London. Famous guests included Mark Twain, Sir Arthur Conan Doyle, and Emperor Louis Napoleon III. During World War II (1939–1945), three bombs damaged the west wing. The cost of operating the hotel became too high.

In 1945, the British Broadcasting Corporation (BBC) bought the building and moved into the hotel. A few guest rooms were used for employees and journalists. That's when the hauntings began.

The Langham has earned its reputation as London's most haunted hotel. BBC employees staying in the building witnessed lots of spooky experiences. From balls of light to a ghost dressed in Victorian fashion, there was no shortage of scares at the Langham.

It reopened as a hotel in 1991. Guests have reported shaking beds, a phantom butler, and cold spots.

After the plane lands, you take a taxi to the hotel. You stare up at the ten-story yellow brick building. Sculptures of griffins, lions, and sphinxes adorn the eaves and window arches. A tower with a pointed dome marks the building's highest point. You've never seen such an impressive building.

Turn the page.

You enter the building through a large stone portico. The lobby opens in front of you, with stone marble columns and polished floors. A chandelier dripping in crystals hangs from the high ceiling.

At the front desk, the clerk smiles and says, "Welcome to the Langham. How can I help you?"

After you give her your name, she types it into the computer. Then her eyes widen. "You're staying in room 333?" she mutters.

You've heard that visitors to room 333 report orbs and a glowing figure of a man. You can't wait to see what the room has in store for you.

"I've heard it's the most haunted room at the hotel," you say. "Are the stories true?"

The clerk hands you the key card to your room. "There are rumors," she says slowly. "But I've never set foot on the third floor. Ghosts freak me out."

As you roll your bag across the floor, a cool breeze gives you goose bumps. *Someone must have come in the front doors*, you think. But when you look, the doors are closed. Shrugging, you ride the elevator to the third floor. Old hotels must get lots of drafts.

Turn the page.

A long hallway with white wall panels stretches out before you. You walk to room 333. You swipe your card, but nothing happens. After more failed attempts, you're about to go downstairs for a new key. But then the lock suddenly clicks, and you push open the door.

Room 333 is small but bright. A window looks down onto the busy streets below. You flop down onto the soft bed. There's nothing scary about this room.

You unpack the ghost-hunting tools you bought for the trip. You hope they'll help you find as many ghoulish former guests as possible. The sun has started going down, and your stomach grumbles. You could set up your equipment now or order a bite to eat first.

- To set up your equipment right away, go to the next page.
- To order something to eat, turn to page 50.

Food can wait. You unpack your new equipment. A notebook and pen are your most important tools. You must jot down everything you see, hear, and feel. Next, you pull out an EMF (electromagnetic field) meter. This tool detects changes in the field caused by ghosts.

You sit on the bed and wait. Room 333 stays pretty quiet. At some point, you drift to sleep. When you wake up, there's a strange light in the corner of the room. Did you leave a lamp on? You rub your eyes and sit up.

The light is an orb! It pulses, getting bigger and bigger. Soon, the light lengthens into the shape of a man. He wears old-time Victorian clothing and stares right at you.

- To turn on your video camera, turn to page 52.
- To try speaking to the ghost, turn to page 53.

You can't concentrate when you're this hungry. You call for room service and order a grilled cheese sandwich. Then you stretch out on the bed and flick on the television.

Soon, there's a soft knocking on the door. That was fast service! You open the door, but there's no one there. You lean into the hall and look both ways. There's no one there.

*Must have been my imagination*, you think.

As you close your door, a butler in a dark suit with polished buttons shuffles down the hall. The butler stops and locks eyes with you.

"Excuse me, sir?" you ask. "Do you know when I can expect my room service order?"

The butler slowly opens his mouth. But instead of answering you, he vanishes! This must be the phantom butler you read about.

You dart back to your room and grab your EMF meter and your phone. The butler might still be lurking somewhere on this floor. Then you remember the ghost of Emperor Louis Napoleon III is said to haunt the basement. His uncle was the famed French military leader Napoleon Bonaparte. Which spooky spirit do you track?

- To roam the hallways looking for the butler, turn to page 58.
- To creep around in the basement, turn to page 70.

You slowly pick up your phone and try to record video. But your phone dies, even though it was fully charged. Fear prickles your neck when you notice the ghost doesn't have any feet or calves. It seems to be standing inside the floor. You reach for your notebook and decide to sketch the ghost instead.

The sounds of a woman crying break your concentration. It's coming from your bathroom. There shouldn't be anyone in there. Your hands grow clammy.

The ghostly figure flickers. You're afraid to blink. The spirit might disappear altogether.

- To stay with the Victorian ghost, go to the next page.
- To investigate the crying in the bathroom, turn to page 68.

The ghost slowly floats toward the bed. Its body almost glows. The room is so cold, you can see your breath.

"Who are you?" you ask. "Why are you here?"

The spirit's head twists at an unnatural angle. Its mouth gapes. Its eyes are black. The ghost reaches toward you. You've encountered a few ghosts in your life. But this one is starting to scare you.

- To try to scare the ghost away, turn to page 54.
- To get a new room, turn to page 56.

Your eyes dart around the room. What could you use as a weapon?

You grab a shoe from the floor and fling it at the ghost. It passes through him and hits the wall. *Thunk!*

The ghost's body twists and contorts, like a marionette doll. Then it fades away completely.

You quickly grab your pencil and write down everything that just happened. This will make an excellent podcast episode. But you're disappointed you couldn't capture the ghost on video.

It's after midnight. You decide to get some sleep. You leave your sound recorder on and snuggle under the covers. Somehow, you're able to fall asleep.

The room's telephone rings and wakes you up. It's 3:33 a.m. This time of night is called the witching hour when paranormal activity is supposed to increase. You pick up the phone and hang it up, but it keeps ringing. It gets louder and starts freaking you out.

- To answer the phone, turn to page 60.
- To hide in the bathroom, turn to page 68.

You rush out of room 333. The hallway is empty. The lights flicker. As you walk toward the elevator, another guest turns a corner. You're relieved to see another living person.

"Thank goodness!" you say.

The man doesn't answer. He continues shuffling toward you. Soon, he is close enough to see his face clearly. A bloody gash on his cheek drips blood.

"Are you okay?" you ask. "Do you need help?"

The man's body flickers, just like the lights. And then he rises above you, floating in midair.

You dash to the staircase and run down the stairs, almost tripping a few times. A different clerk is working the front desk. You grab the desk, trying to catch your breath. Then you tell the clerk about your ghostly encounters.

"You've met two of the Langham's most famous ghosts," he says. "The Victorian man is a doctor. Legend says he murdered his wife here at the hotel. It was their honeymoon."

You shiver. "What about the man with the bloody face?"

The clerk shrugs. "No one knows who he is. But he's been spotted all over the hotel. Poor fellow. Would you like to check into a different room? Room 632 is available. Though we've heard tales from that room too."

You're embarrassed you ran so quickly. What would your listeners think? But now you're curious about this new room. You can only afford one night at the hotel. You must choose wisely.

- To check in to room 632, turn to page 62.
- To return to room 333, turn to page 64.

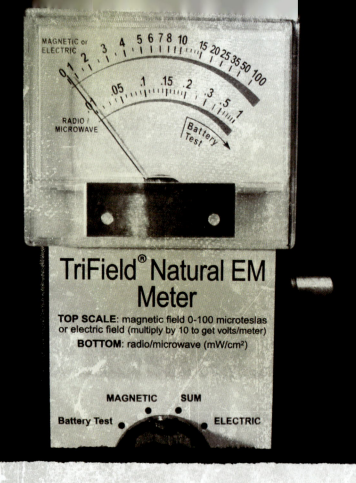

As you move slowly up and down the hallway, you hold out your EMF meter. But it doesn't register any spirits. The hall is quiet. Almost too quiet.

Perhaps you'll have more luck in the basement. As you near the elevators, the lights on your meter begin blinking. Are you close to finding another ghost?

A man wearing a military uniform rounds the corner. You freeze. The man's jacket is buttoned up to his neck. Several medals are pinned to it. His body is almost see-through as he marches toward you.

You hold up your phone to snap a photo, but your shaky hands drop it. You bend down to pick it up. You look up in time to see the spirit pass through a closed door!

- To follow the ghost, turn to page 66.
- To continue to the basement, turn to page 70.

You nervously pick up the phone.

"Hello?" you ask, trembling. But there's only static on the other end of the line. You hang up, but it rings again. Again, you pick up the phone. Again, there's only static.

The third time it rings, you unplug the phone and shove it into a dresser drawer. Your eyes dart around the room. You're too wide awake to even try to fall asleep.

The phone rings.

"I'm out of here," you say and quickly pack your things. You want your podcast to be a hit. But first, you have to survive the night at the Langham!

Crossing the room, you grab the knob. But it won't turn. Goose bumps break out on your arms. You have a bad feeling about this.

You hear breathing behind you. An invisible hand curls around one shoulder. You let out a terrible scream and collapse to the floor.

When you wake up, it's morning. You rush from the room, not bothering to grab your stuff. In the lobby, nothing is as you remember. The decor is darker and older. All the people are dressed in old-time clothing.

A porter stops you at the main door. He's dressed in blue and wears a powdered wig. "Where do you think you're going?" he asks. "No one leaves the Langham before checkout."

You push past him and stumble out the revolving door. But instead of finding yourself out on the street, you're back in room 333.

## THE END

To follow another path, turn to page 15.
To learn more about haunted hotels, turn to page 101.

You unlock the door to room 632. A porter has already delivered your things to the room. You wonder what new spirits you might encounter here. After you set up all your equipment again, you settle onto the bed.

Hours pass, and nothing happens. Maybe you made a mistake checking into this room. But it's too late now. You change into your pajamas and brush your teeth. At least you had some haunting experiences in room 333. It's better than nothing.

You drift off to sleep. Suddenly, you're jolted awake. The mattress shakes. But there's no one else in the room. You scream. The lights flash on and off as the shaking grows more violent. The mattress turns sideways, and you topple onto the floor. You land on your shoulder and feel something snap.

"Help!" you cry out in pain. You dial for help, and soon an ambulance arrives. Your night at the Langham Hotel has ended painfully early.

## THE END

To follow another path, turn to page 15.
To learn more about haunted hotels, turn to page 101.

Room 333 is a paranormal hot spot. You gather your courage and return to the room. It's empty. You double check to make sure all your equipment is working. Then you sit on the bed and wait.

You don't have to wait long. The pulsing ball of light appears again in the corner of your room. Soon, it morphs into the ghostly Victorian man.

"Are you a doctor?" you ask.

He slowly nods. You can't believe a ghost is communicating with you!

"Did you come to the Langham Hotel on your honeymoon?"

The ghost throws its head back. Its jaws unhinge, and it lets out an inhuman screech. The curtains shred. The television falls to the floor. You duck down as your equipment smashes against the walls. The last thing you remember before you faint is the ghost's twisted face.

When you wake up, sunlight streams in through the curtains. The room is clean. Your equipment is just fine. Was it all just a nightmare? Dream or not, you can't wait to check out of the Langham.

## THE END

To follow another path, turn to page 15.
To learn more about haunted hotels, turn to page 101.

You hurry to the door and turn the handle. It's unlocked. You slowly ease it open.

This room is not like the others. The carpet is darker. Dark floral wallpaper covers the walls. There's no television. Music plays from a wooden box on the dresser. But it's unlike any music you've ever heard.

Suddenly, the ghost appears at an open window.

"Hello?" you ask. "Are you alright?

The spirit turns to look at you. He speaks in another language. You can't understand him, but he seems upset. Then he leaps out the window.

"Stop!" you shout. But it's too late. When you look out the window, the man is gone.

You return to your room. You must have encountered the ghost of the German prince you read about. You feel sad for this man and decide to do more research about his life. His story could make a great addition to your next podcast episode.

When you slip under the covers, your feet bump into something cold and hard. You whip back the covers. Lying in the sheets is an antique war medal.

## THE END

To follow another path, turn to page 15.
To learn more about haunted hotels, turn to page 101.

You hurry into the bathroom and close the door behind you. You can feel a presence in the room. As your eyes adjust to the dark, your muscles tense. A woman in an old-fashioned bridal gown hovers near the sink. Her body is see-through, and her eyes are silver.

"Help," she cries.

"How?" you ask. She holds a bouquet of white flowers. But their petals have started to wilt.

"My groom," she says. "Don't let him find me!"

Is she speaking about the Victorian ghost in room 333? Suddenly, the bathroom door handle shakes violently. You jam your shoulder against the door. But you're losing strength.

Finally, the door bursts open. Your body is flung backward. You hit your head on the sink. Everything goes black.

When you wake up, you're in the hospital. The back of your head aches. You hope the pain will be worth it when your first podcast episode drops.

## THE END

To follow another path, turn to page 15.
To learn more about haunted hotels, turn to page 101.

Basements can be spooky places. But this basement isn't creepy at all. It's been turned into a luxury spa. You doubt you'll find any ghosts down here.

When you get to the pool room, you're the only one there. It is almost midnight. You didn't realize it was so late. The room is silent. You settle into a pool chair. Soon, the EMF device starts flashing.

A man enters. It's hard to see him from where you sit on the other end of the room. He appears to have a large mustache. He also wears a regal coat. Could it be the ghost of French Emperor Napoleon III? You know he lived at the Langham before his death in 1873.

The man leaves the room. You hurry to the door and throw it open. A man stands with his back to you.

With a shaking voice you say, "Emperor?"

The man turns. "I'm sorry?" he says, quizzically.

Your eyes dart to his jacket. He wears a name tag. He's a hotel worker, not the emperor.

"Sorry." You shake your head, embarrassed. You must have imagined your ghostly encounter with Napoleon III.

## THE END

To follow another path, turn to page 15.
To learn more about haunted hotels, turn to page 101.

# CHAPTER 4
# THE FAIRMONT BANFF SPRINGS HOTEL

You're traveling by train with Molly and her family to Banff, Alberta, Canada. Nestled in the Rocky Mountains, the Fairmont Banff Springs Hotel looks like a castle.

You spend much of the train ride learning more about the hotel. The Fairmont Banff Springs Hotel was opened in 1888 by the Canadian Pacific Railway. In 1939, England's King George VI and his wife stayed there. The hotel is also famous for its ghostly activity. It puts on ghost tours every Halloween.

Turn the page.

The train pulls into the station. Molly's aunt Winifred puts on her black cape and gloves. She told you lots of stories about the hotel's alleged hauntings.

"I haven't been here since I was a girl," she says, gathering her bag. "If all my old spooky pals show up, your podcast will be a hit!"

Everyone boards a bus for a quick ride to the hotel. When you arrive, snow covers the trees. The building looks like a fairy tale. Several stories of red-brown stone soar above you.

Inside the lobby, elevator doors are tucked into more stone walls. At the front desk, everyone gets their keys. You and Molly are sharing a room. A young bellhop helps carry your bags up the stairs.

"Is it true the hotel is haunted?" you ask.

"I've never seen any ghosts," he admits. "But there are rumors."

Molly nudges you with her elbow. "Legend says room 873 was closed off after a family died there," she whispers. The idea of finding the room both terrifies and thrills you.

After you and Molly unpack, there's a knock at your door. It's Molly's parents and Aunt Winifred. They invite you to dinner at the hotel restaurant. Molly joins them in the castle-like hallway. Sconces on the walls give off a dim light.

"You coming?" she asks.

A meal does sound good. But you're also tired and want to take a nap.

- To rest for a bit, turn to page 76.
- To head to the restaurant with Molly and her family, turn to page 77.

It's softly snowing outside your window as you turn off the lights and snuggle under the covers. The bellhop's story about a closed-off guest room plays on a loop in your mind. It sounds like the plot of a scary movie! If you can find the room, your podcast episode is sure to be a hit.

Sleepiness overtakes you, and you drift off. Soon, a scratching sound wakes you. It almost sounds like fingernails clawing the wall. When you open your eyes, it stops. But all the lights are on. You know you turned them off before your nap. Maybe Molly stopped in the room while you were sleeping and turned them on. She could have forgotten something. You're still sleepy, but you're not sure you want to stay alone in this room any longer.

- To join the others at the restaurant, go to the next page.
- To try to fall back asleep, turn to page 84.

The Fairmont Banff Springs Hotel has several restaurants. You join Molly and her family in the fancy French restaurant.

"These views are incredible," you say as you take the empty chair next to Aunt Winifred. "The mountains are beautiful."

Winifred gives you a knowing look. "Meet any ghostly visitors yet?"

"Stop it, Aunt Winnie," Molly says. "Food first, then ghost talk."

You feast on a meal of chicken cooked with bacon, butter, and mushrooms. Afterward, Molly's family heads to the pool. You and Molly decide to explore the hotel for a while. It's so big, it would take hours to see every nook and cranny. And you're hoping to scare up a ghost or two.

Turn the page.

As you tour the rambling hotel, you're struck by its grandeur. Velvet wing-backed chairs sit in front of giant windows, overlooking the snow-covered Rockies. Massive chandeliers soar over multiple ballrooms. You can imagine this place a hundred years ago, filled with dancing guests. You wish you could travel back in time and see it for yourself.

The Fairmont has many hallways and staircases. As you pass one, Molly grabs your arm.

"Look!" she says, pointing at a curved marble staircase.

A woman stands at the top of the stairs. She wears a long, white bridal gown. An intricate veil hangs down her back.

"There must be a wedding here today," you say.

Molly is obsessed with reality TV wedding shows. "Let's go check it out," she says.

The bride stands perfectly still, as if frozen in a portrait. A feeling of unease slithers up your spine.

- To follow Molly up the stairs, turn to page 80.
- To keep exploring on your own, turn to page 82.

Molly leads the way up the staircase. The higher you climb, the chillier the air feels. Maybe it's the snowstorm outside. There must be a draft.

The top of the staircase opens into a grand ballroom. Pillars of polished marble rise to the high ceiling. A grand piano sits off to one side.

But the room is empty. The bride is gone, and there are no guests.

"Guess she went somewhere else," you say. "Let's leave."

"Wait," Molly says. "I see her over by the window."

She moves toward the bride without another word. Her sneakers squeak against the floor.

You start to follow, but then you notice a flickering light on the staircase behind you.

*That's strange,* you think. Something about that light gives you a bad feeling.

- To approach the bride with Molly, turn to page 91.
- To investigate the light, turn to page 98.

You explore more of the hotel on your own. The Fairmont Banff Springs Hotel is like a small city packed into one building. There are dozens of shops and restaurants. You stop at one to buy some chocolate.

You ride the elevator to one of the higher floors. Gold-framed paintings adorn the hall. A light on the wall suddenly goes out.

*It's probably just a bad bulb,* you tell yourself.

Up ahead, an older man in a plaid bellhop's uniform struggles with some luggage.

"Can I help you?" you ask.

The man smiles. His gray hair is combed perfectly to one side.

"I'd be glad for some help," he says in a Scottish accent. "I'm Sam."

You shake his hand and introduce yourself. Then you pick up a suitcase. It's made of old leather.

"What room are we taking these to?" you ask.

"Room 873," he says, and your skin grows cold. Isn't that the room that was allegedly boarded over? You're about to ask Sam what happened in that room. But when you turn toward him, he's gone.

"Sam?" you call out. "Where'd you go?" You're still holding the suitcase.

- To look for room 873, turn to 85.
- To return to your room, turn to page 89.

You read that the original hotel burned down in 1926. It was built of wood. The current hotel reopened in 1928. Perhaps the fire affected the hotel's wiring. Or maybe you were so tired you only imagined turning off the lights.

Yawning, you turn off the lights and crawl back into bed. You just need an hour or two of rest. Then you can unlock the ghostly secrets of the Fairmont.

The sounds of bloodcurdling screams shatter the peaceful silence. You sit up in bed, eyes searching the dark. Your heart beats so fast you feel as though you might faint. The screams are coming from inside the room!

- To run into the hall, turn to page 93.
- To turn on the lights, turn to page 95.

You decide to find room 873 on your own. As you ride the elevator up to the eighth floor, you text Molly. You tell her about the mysterious bellhop and the missing room. When you get to the eighth floor, you wait for her. You can barely hold still, you're so excited. This mystery is screaming at you to solve it.

The elevator doors ding open, and Molly steps off. You're both quiet as you move down the hall. Soon, you find rooms 872 and 874. But room 873 is curiously missing. You go up and down the hall again, just to be sure you didn't miss it. But there is no room 873.

"The room should be right here," you say. You touch a plain wall where the door should be. The wall feels like ice. Before you can take your hand away, you're tumbling forward.

Turn the page.

You find yourself standing inside a hotel room. But it's not decorated like your room. The room looks old-fashioned. There isn't even a television.

Seated at a round table are two adults and a young girl. The woman wears a long, vintage dress. The man has on suspenders and dress pants. The girl has a book in her hands.

"You must be the bellhop," the woman says. Then she points to the suitcase you're still holding for Sam. "That's our bag."

You look down to find you're wearing a plaid bellhop uniform. It's the same uniform Sam wore. Your hands get clammy, and you quickly set down the bag. This must be the family that died in this room. You stumble to the door, wishing there was a way to save this family.

Turn the page.

You end up back in the hallway where Molly waits for you. But for some reason, you're lying on the ground.

"Are you okay?" she asks. "The moment you touched the wall, you fainted!"

You tell her your incredible story. Was it just a dream? Or did you stumble upon the ghosts of room 873? Molly helps you up. As you walk away, you realize you're not holding the suitcase anymore. You look around, but it's nowhere to be found.

## THE END

To follow another path, turn to page 15.
To learn more about haunted hotels, turn to page 101.

You set the suitcase down and walk to one end of the hall and back. But Sam the bellhop isn't there. There was something strange about him. And now you're getting a headache. You decide to drop the suitcase at the front desk before heading to your room. Only when you return to where you set it, the bag is gone.

*Another bellhop must have taken it,* you try to convince yourself.

You return to your empty room. You try to text Molly, but your phone doesn't have any service. You set your phone down and crawl into bed. You're exhausted.

Suddenly, the pillow is yanked out from underneath your head. It flies across the room and lands on the floor.

"Molly?" you say. But there's no one here.

Turn the page.

"Hello?" you call. When unseen hands push you, you run screaming from the room. You can't spend another second in there alone.

You bump into Winifred in the hall. "No need to explain," she says calmly. "That's the same room I stayed in as a girl. I didn't get a wink of sleep. Those mischievous ghosts would not let me be."

"Do you know who haunts that room?" you ask. Your voice shakes, and your pulse drums in your ears.

"I'm afraid not, dear," Winifred says. "But that's half the fun!"

You're not sure you agree. But at least your podcast episode won't be boring!

## THE END

To follow another path, turn to page 15.
To learn more about haunted hotels, turn to page 101.

You follow Molly across the ballroom. She stops at one of the large windows. The bride stands at the window, gazing outside. She seems sad.

"Are you alright?" you ask. Maybe she's nervous about her wedding.

The bride doesn't answer. Instead, she whisks past you to the center of the ballroom. She starts dancing, as if with an invisible partner.

You and Molly exchange confused glances. "This is so weird," you whisper. Molly agrees.

Something clangs behind you. A worker pushes a mop and bucket to the center of the ballroom. He starts washing the floors.

When you turn back toward the bride, she's gone. You and Molly search the room, but she seems to have vanished.

Turn the page.

You approach the worker. "Excuse me," you say. "When does the wedding start?"

The man gives you an odd look. "There are no weddings booked for this weekend."

"But what about the bride?" Molly asks. "She was just here."

The worker puts his mop in the bucket. "Back in the 1920s, a bride accidentally fell down the stairs and died. People often report her ghost on the stairs and dancing in this ballroom."

As he continues mopping, you and Molly return to the staircase. You can almost see a shadowy figure floating down them. When you blink, it's gone.

## THE END

To follow another path, turn to page 15.
To learn more about haunted hotels, turn to page 101.

Can ghosts scream? You don't bother turning on the lights or getting your shoes. You barrel into the hallway and almost crash into a bellhop. He has gray hair and wears a plaid uniform. The bellhop you met earlier that day wore a more modern uniform.

"Can I help you with something?" the man asks. He has a Scottish accent. "I'm Sam."

You nod. "I heard terrible screaming in my room. But no one else is in there."

"Let me help you to the lobby, and we'll get this all straightened out," Sam says. He walks you to the lobby. "The front desk clerk will fix everything," he promises you.

"Thank you, Sam. I really appreciate your help."

Turn the page.

"That's what I'm here for." He smiles and goes into another room.

At the front desk, you tell the clerk about the screaming in your room. "I'm so glad Sam was there to help me," you say.

The clerk makes a strange face. "Was he wearing a plaid uniform? Spoke with a Scottish accent?"

"Yes," you say slowly. "Is there a problem?"

"A man named Sam McCauley worked at the hotel as a bellhop," she says. "But I'm afraid he died more than 40 years ago."

## THE END

To follow another path, turn to page 15.
To learn more about haunted hotels, turn to page 101.

With trembling hands, you turn on the bedside lamp. The screaming stops. But the scene before you looks like something out of a horror movie.

Bloody handprints cover the walls and mirror. Panic builds inside your chest. Just as you're about to scream, the door to your room opens. You brace yourself for whatever nightmare is about to enter.

Molly steps inside. "What's wrong?" she asks.

You tell her about the screaming and the bloody handprints. But when you look around, the handprints are gone.

"I swear they were just here!" you insist. Did you only imagine them?

"I believe you," Molly says. "Let's stay up late and see if anything else spooky happens. It'll be great for your podcast."

She helps set up your sound recorder and video camera. Her presence is calming. Together, you wait for the ghosts of the Fairmont Banff Springs Hotel to return.

# THE END

To follow another path, turn to page 15.
To learn more about haunted hotels, turn to page 101.

You move slowly back toward the stairs. Dozens of small lit candles line each side of the staircase. These weren't here a moment ago. You bend closer to one. When you blow on it, the flame doesn't move.

"Can I help you with anything?" a voice asks.

Startled, you stand up quickly. A hotel worker waits just below you on the stairs. When you look around, the candles have vanished.

"There were candles on the stairs," you explain. "But now they're gone. Does this happen often?"

She nods. "You're not the first guest to report the ghostly candles. Long ago, a bride was walking up these stairs. Her dress brushed one of the lit candles, and the fabric caught on fire. Tragically, she fell down the stairs and died. Her ghost never left."

# THE END

To follow another path, turn to page 15.
To learn more about haunted hotels, turn to page 101.

The Crescent Hotel and Spa

# CHAPTER 5
# HAUNTED HOTELS

A hotel is like a home away from home. All sorts of people check in and check out. These places have seen a lot of history, including deaths. This might explain why so many hotels around the world are said to be haunted. But are any of the ghost stories true?

Several people died at the Crescent Hotel when it was a hospital. In 1940, Norman Baker was convicted of mail fraud for sending false advertising about his cancer cure. He closed his hospital and spent several years in prison. The Crescent reopened as a hotel in the late 1940s.

In 2019, hotel staff made a grisly discovery. They found old jars and bottles buried on the Crescent Hotel property. Testing of the jars is ongoing. They might contain tissue from some of Baker's patients.

At the Langham Hotel, history might confirm one ghostly sighting. In room 333, the Victorian ghost is often described as standing inside the floor. Its feet and calves aren't visible. The floors in the guest rooms were raised when heating ducts were installed. Does this prove the ghost is real?

The ghost bride at the Fairmont Banff Springs Hotel is the hotel's most famous spirit. But rumors swirl that hotel staff invented the story. Other hauntings, however, are rooted in truth. A bellhop named Sam McCauley really did work at the Fairmont. Stories say Sam promised to haunt the hotel after he died.

Many guests have had ghostly experiences at the Crescent, Langham, and Fairmont hotels. From strange noises to cold spots to full apparitions, visitors swear the hauntings are true. Each hotel has gained a haunting reputation. Many visitors check in already knowing the spooky tales. Might this make them more likely to have a ghostly encounter?

# MORE GHOSTLY ENCOUNTERS

A footman is said to haunt one of the Langham Hotel's guest rooms. Witnesses say the ghost wears a powdered wig. Before the hotel was built, a house stood on the property. This footman may have worked at that house.

A fancy ghost haunts the Crescent Hotel. The ghost has been reported on the staircase or at the bar. He wears a tuxedo, top hat, and white gloves. Some people think it might be the ghost of Dr. Ellis. He was the hotel doctor when it was originally opened.

The ghost bride is the Fairmont Banff Springs Hotel's most famous haunted guest. She has appeared on a Canadian stamp. Other reported hauntings include a ghost child that appears in a window. People have also witnessed a headless man playing the bagpipes and a phantom bartender.

# OTHER PATHS TO EXPLORE

Some people research ghosts for their jobs. They make podcasts, write books, and even host television shows. But lots of ordinary people have ghostly sightings too. What would you do if you encountered a ghost? Would you tell others about your experience?

Sam the bellman didn't die at the Fairmont Banff Springs Hotel. Do you believe his ghost really returned to his former job? Or might there be another reason the story of Sam the ghost is so popular?

Would you work at an allegedly haunted hotel? Imagine the hotel you work at has never had any actual hauntings. The hotel manager invented the stories to draw more guests. Part of your job is to talk about the ghosts with the guests. Would you feel comfortable telling made-up ghost stories?

# GLOSSARY

**cancer** (KAN-suhr)—a serious disease in which some cells in the body grow faster than normal cells

**convicted** (kahn-VIK-tuhd)—describes a person found guilty of a crime

**electromagnetic field** (i-lek-troh-mag-NET-ik FEELD)—a field of force created by moving electric charges

**morgue** (MORG)—a place where dead bodies are kept at a hospital

**paranormal** (pair-uh-NOR-muhl)—having to do with an unexplained event that has no scientific explanation

**phantom** (FAN-tuhm)—something that appears to be real but is not, like a ghost

**scaffolding** (SKAF-ol-ding)—temporary framework or set of platforms used to support workers and materials

**specimen** (SPESS-uh-muhn)—a sample that a scientist studies closely

**X-ray** (EKS-ray)—a photograph of the inside of a person's body

# BIBLIOGRAPHY

Crain, Mary Beth. *Haunted Pet Stories: Tales of Ghostly Cats, Spooky Dogs, and Demonic Bunnies.* Essex, CT: Globe Pequot, 2011.

Fowler, Gene, and Bill Crawford. *Border Radio: Quacks, Yodelers, Pitchmen, Psychics, and other Amazing Broadcasters of the American Airwaves.* Austin, TX: University of Texas Press, 2002.

Ogden, Tom. *Haunted Hotels: Eerie Inns, Ghoulish Guests, and Creepy Caretakers.* Guilford, CT: Globe Pequot, 2022.

Pickup, Gilly. *Haunted West End.* Stroud, England: The History Press, 2013.

Robinson, Bart. *Banff Springs: The Story of a Hotel.* Banff, AB, Canada: Summerthought Pub., 2007.

# READ MORE

Emminizer, Theresa. *The Ghostly Guide to the Queen Mary*. Buffalo, NY: Gareth Stevens Publishing, 2024.

Peterson, Megan Cooley. *Salem's Spirits and Other Hauntings of New England*. North Mankato, MN: Capstone Press, a Capstone Imprint, 2021.

Troupe, Thomas Kingsley. *Haunted Hotels*. New York: Crabtree Publishing Company, 2022.

# INTERNET SITES

*1886 Crescent Hotel & Spa*
crescent-hotel.com/about/history/

*History of the BBC: The Langham*
bbc.com/historyofthebbc/buildings/the-langham

*Scary Ghost Facts for Kids—Boo!*
kidpillar.com/ghost-facts-for-kids/

# ABOUT THE AUTHOR

Megan Cooley Peterson is a children's book author and editor. When not writing, Megan enjoys movies, books, and all things Halloween. She lives in Minnesota with her husband and daughter.